NOLAN

Bible Story

Puppet Skits Kids Can Do

24 Quick and Easy Scripts for Ages 8 to 12

SONJA ZIEGLER

STANDARD PUBLISHING

Cincinnati, Ohio

GANOCI

Edited by Theresa C. Hayes
Cover and inside design by Diana Walters

All Scripture quotations, unless otherwise indicated, are quoted from the International Children's Bible, New
Century Version, copyright © 1986, 1988 by Word Publishing,
Dallas, Texas, 75039. Used by permission.

Standard Publishing, Cincinnati, Ohio.
A division of Standex International Corporation.

07 06 05 04 03 02 01 00   5 4 3 2 1

Contents

TIPS FOR USING PUPPETS

Basic Entrances and Exits

Unless the script states otherwise, puppets should always enter the puppet stage area as though walking up steps and exit as though walking down steps. Occasionally a script will call for peeking over the stage, or floating in, or popping up and down. But otherwise, use the step method.

Hand and Arm Movement

There are various types of puppets used in children's ministry today. One of the most commonly used is the rod-arm puppet where the puppeteer operates the mouth with one hand and with the other hand, moves a rod attached to the puppet's arm in order to make additional movements called for in the skit (i.e. hold up a note or other object, make gestures, etc.). The skits in this book have been written especially with the use of rod-arm puppets in mind, but can easily be adapted to work with all puppet types.

Expressions and Other Human Traits

Sleeping: Puppets have eyes that do not close. So if you want to show someone sleeping, you must lay the puppet's head on the top of the stage in such a way that its eyes are not visible to the audience.

Praying: To pray, have the puppet bow its head and either cover its eyes with its hand, or bend your wrist so far that the puppet is looking at the floor and its eyes are not easily seen. You can even rest the puppet's head face down on the stage to keep its eyes from being shown.

Laughter: Open the puppet's mouth and tilt its head back; move the head up and down while laughing.

Whistling or Humming: Whistling is hard since puppets don't pucker. If you must whistle, just open the puppet's mouth slightly. Humming is easier and you can do this while the puppet's mouth is closed or just slightly open.

Surprise: To show surprise, open the puppet's mouth suddenly while you gasp. You can also show surprise by clasping the puppet's hand over its mouth.

Sadness: This expression is best shown by having the puppet look down and put its hand to its head. Keep its mouth closed unless it is speaking.

Anger: Anger can be displayed by having the puppet shake while making angry sounds or saying something that displays its anger.

Costumes, Props, and Special Effects

The key in puppetry is to show rather than tell. Anytime you can create action and show the story or truth you are trying to convey, the better your performance will be! Always look for ways to enhance skits through the use of costumes, props, unusual sounds, lighting, and other special effects such as bubbles and water sprinkles. Also, involve the audience as much as possible in what's going on!

Divine Assignment

Scripture: Matthew 1

Characters: Angel 1, Angel 2

Costumes/Props:
- Both puppets should be wearing white with halos. (Halos can be made from gold or white chenille wires formed into circles and attached to the puppets' heads.)
- Audio cassette of praise music (optional)

——— Script ———

Angel 1 enters singing praise song—either a cappella or to audio cassette. After he has sung for a few seconds, Angel 2 enters in a hurry.

Angel 2: Oh, there you are! I've been looking all over for you!

Angel 1: *[stops singing and turns toward Angel 2. If using audio cassette, fade music.]* Yes? What is it?

Angel 2: God wants you to go to earth right away on a very important assignment! I was sent to find you and fill you in on the details!

Angel 1: An important assignment? This is great! What do I need to do?

Angel 2: Well, you've already heard about the problems . . .

Angel 1: *[sadly]* Yes—the sin. I've been on missions to earth before and I've seen the results. It's absolutely terrible!

Angel 2: Yes. It's quite depressing. But the good news is that God has devised a brilliant plan to provide a way out—a way that people can be set free from their sin!

Angel 1: That's incredible! What's the plan?

Angel 2: *[pause]* He's going to send his Son down there to save them.

Angel 1: *[shocked]* What?

Angel 2: Yes. In fact, his Son is going to be there for a number of earth years and will live among them as a human being.

Angel 1: You mean—?

Angel 2: Yes. He will experience everything that they do: sadness, pain, loneliness . . .

Angel 1:	Wow—that sure is a lot to ask of him! Why would he want to leave all this peace and beauty in Heaven and go to earth? I sure wouldn't want to live down there!
Angel 2:	He's going because he loves them—even with all their faults. Even with all their sin! And he wants to save them from their sin.
Angel 1:	This is amazing! How can I help?
Angel 2:	Well, God has chosen two people to help begin his plan—Mary and Joseph of Nazareth. Gabriel has already visited Mary to tell her that, through the power of the Holy Spirit, she will give birth to God's Son.
Angel 1:	Wow! How'd she handle the news?
Angel 2:	It amazed her to be sure! But now we've got to get word to Joseph! You see, Joseph and Mary are engaged to be married, and he's not handling the news too well. In fact, he's planning to call off the wedding! We must make sure that does not happen! *[Pause.]* And that's where you come in.
Angel 1:	What do I need to do?
Angel 2:	You must visit him tonight and tell him not to be afraid to marry her. Tell him that what Mary said is true—she is going to have a baby who is the Son of God!
Angel 1:	Yes, yes—is there anything else?
Angel 2:	Tell him that the baby's name will be Jesus—which means salvation. Tell him that Jesus will save his people from their sins. Got it?
Angel 1:	Got it! I will leave tonight! This is an amazing plan! God must really love them a lot!
Angel 2:	Yes, it is quite a sacrifice to send his own beloved Son. But he feels it is worth it. Now hurry and get ready—it's almost time to go!
Angel 1:	OK. *[Turns to leave, moves a step or two, then turns back.]*
Angel 2:	What is it?
Angel 1:	*[pause]* I just hope that the people on earth will realize what this means.
Angel 2:	*[nods]* So do I. *[As Angel 1 exits:]* So do I.

Digging Deeper

If you had been friends with Mary, would it have been difficult for you to believe that she was going to give birth to God's Son?

Is it sometimes hard to believe that God will use an ordinary person like you or me?

Name some ways Jesus experienced the same problems we experience (sadness, pain, etc.).

The Incredible View

Scripture: Luke 5:17-26

Characters: Jonathan, Michael

Props/Costumes:
- Pair of toy binoculars attached to Jonathan's hand with tape (small binoculars can be purchased at a toy or variety store—or you can make a pair by taping two empty toilet paper tubes together)
- Small lunch sack taped to Michael's arm

Script

Jonathan enters and looks through binoculars. After a few seconds, Michael enters.

Michael: Oh, there you are, Jonathan! There are so many people down there, I thought I'd never get through! *[Looks around.]* How'd you ever find this spot way up here?

Jonathan: *[lowers binoculars and turns toward Michael]* I've known about this place for a while. It's called "Lookout Point." Isn't this a great view of the city? I figured since we couldn't get into the house where Jesus is teaching, we'd at least be able to get a glimpse of him from here—as soon as he comes out!

Michael: I wonder what he looks like. I've heard some really amazing stories about him!

Jonathan: *[still looking through binoculars]* We'll find out soon enough. I can see the house clearly from here.

Michael: Has anything exciting happened yet?

Jonathan: Not really—only a whole lot of people trying to fit into that tiny little house! I'll bet there are a couple hundred people down there!

Michael: *[sighs]* I wish I had some binoculars too.

Jonathan: *[still looking through binoculars]* Oh my goodness! I don't believe it!

Michael: *[excited]* What is it?

Jonathan: Some of the guys from town are bringing Josiah in on a stretcher! There's Peter, and Jacob—and Nat!

Michael: They must be taking him to Jesus! Nat told me that Jesus can actually heal people!

Jonathan: Yeah—but Jesus doesn't know that Josiah's been paralyzed for years—ever since he fell off his roof!

Michael: I wish we could get into that house to see what's happening!

Jonathan: It doesn't look like they're going to get in! They can't get through the crowd. *[Lowers binoculars.]* Well, I'm beginning to think that this wasn't such a great idea. Who knows how long Jesus will be in there! We should have brought something to eat.

Michael: Hey! I did bring us something to eat— *[holds up lunch sack]* some peanut butter and banana sandwiches!

Jonathan: That was good thinking, Michael—I'm getting hungry!

Michael: Hey—what's all the commotion down there?

Jonathan: *[looks through binoculars again]* Oh my goodness! This is incredible! The guys have taken off part of the roof—and they are lowering Josiah down into the house on the stretcher!

Michael: Can you see anything inside the house?

Jonathan: No. Too many people. *[Pause.]* Wait! I think I see something!

Michael: *[excited]* What's happening?! Do you see him?

Jonathan: No—nothing yet. Wait—someone's coming out of the house! *[Excited—his voice getting louder.]* It's Josiah! He's walking out of the house! And that must be Jesus beside him! *[Lowers binoculars and looks at Michael—they stare at each other a moment; then both jump up and down while cheering.]*

Both: Yea! Whooohoo! Yahoo! *[Cheer for a few seconds.]*

Jonathan: *[looks at Michael]* That is incredible! Can you believe it? Jesus healed Josiah!

Michael: Yeah! It looks like the stories we've been hearing about Jesus doing miracles are true—and we just saw one! Do you think he really is the Son of God?

Jonathan: After what we just saw, how can you doubt it? Come on! Let's go hear what he has to say! *[Jonathan exits.]*

Michael: Yeah! I want to hear what the Son of God has to say! Hey! Wait for me! *[Exits after Jonathan.]*

Digging Deeper

If you had lived when Jesus was on earth, would it have been hard for you to believe that he is the Son of God?

Why did seeing Jesus do miracles help some people to believe that he is God's Son?

Why did some people still not believe in him, even after they saw miracles?

How can we help people today see that Jesus is the Son of God?

Do You Have an Appointment?

Scripture: Mark 10:13-16

Characters: Danny, Sarah, Peter and John (two of Jesus' disciples), Jesus

Props/Costumes:
- All wear biblical dress.

—— Script ——

Peter and John enter and face each other stage right, moving mouths silently as if talking. After a moment Danny and Sarah enter from stage left and approach them.

Danny: Excuse me, sir?

Peter and John turn to face the kids.

Peter: Yes? What is it?

Danny: Are you him?

Peter: Am I who?

Sarah: Jesus. Are you Jesus?

Peter: *[chuckles]* Heh, heh, heh. Not even close!

Danny: *[to John]* Are you, sir? Are you Jesus?

John: What? No, I'm not Jesus. What are you kids doing here anyway? Shouldn't you be in school or something?

Sarah: *[excited]* We came to see Jesus!

Danny: *[happy]* We want to meet him!

Peter: Well, do you have an appointment?

Danny: *[disappointed]* An appointment? We have to have an appointment?

Peter: Now listen kids, Jesus is a very busy man!

John: *[nodding]* Very busy.

Peter: And he has only so many hours in a day—

John:	—to preach and teach and do miracles!
Peter:	And there are a lot of important people over there *[motion with arm to stage right]* who have been waiting all day to speak with him!
John:	So you kids just run along home and play or something, OK?

Both turn away from kids and remark to each other:

Peter:	Kids, eh?
John:	Yeah!

Peter and John continue facing toward stage right.

Danny:	*[to Sarah]* Phooey! I really wanted to meet him.
Sarah:	Or at least get to see him!
Danny:	*[sadly]* I guess he only talks to grown-ups.
Sarah:	Yeah. Let's go.

Both turn to leave toward stage left and then Jesus enters facing them.

Jesus:	*[kindly]* Hello, children.
Danny:	*[glum]* Oh, hi.
Jesus:	Is something wrong?
Sarah:	Well, we came to see Jesus. We wanted to meet him—but he's too busy to see us.
Danny:	Yeah, those other guys said we can't meet him 'cause he has more important people waiting to see him!
Jesus:	Well, I'm sorry they said that, because it's just not true. You are just as important to me as anyone here—and I'd be happy to talk to you!
Sarah:	*[stammering]* You? You would be happy to . . . you, you are—I mean, you're—
Danny:	Jesus?! You're Jesus?! Really?!
Jesus:	Yes, I am. What would you like to talk about?

Peter and John turn and see kids with Jesus and rush toward them.

Peter:	Hey! I thought we told you kids to run along home!
John:	Can't you see Jesus is very busy?! Now, scoot!

Jesus:	Wait a minute! These children came to talk to me! Don't send them away!
Peter:	But Jesus—
Jesus:	*[to Peter and John]* The Kingdom of God belongs to people who are like these little children. Don't ever stop them from coming to see me! *[Puts his arms around Danny and Sarah as they exit.]* Now, what was it you wanted to talk about?
Peter:	*[watches them exit]* I guess we made a mistake.
John:	Yeah. We should have realized that Jesus will always have time for kids—he always has time for everyone!
Peter:	Yeah. *[Pause.]* Well, we won't make that mistake again! Come on, buddy, let's go see about some dinner.
John:	Great idea!

Peter and John exit together.

Digging Deeper

Why do you think the disciples wouldn't help the children meet Jesus?

Have you ever felt as though grown-ups didn't have time to talk with you?

How does it make you feel to know that Jesus always has time for you?

How can we show Jesus that we are thankful for his love?

Dangerous Decision

Scripture: Daniel 6

Characters: Joe (first soldier), Pete (second soldier), Daniel

Props/Costumes:
- Both soldiers wear armor and carry swords over their shoulders like rifles.

———— Script ————

Joe enters stage right, on guard duty. He begins marching stage left.

Joe: Hut, two, three, four *[turns in opposite direction]*. Hut, two, three, four *[turns in opposite direction]*.

After Joe turns, Pete enters behind him from stage right.

Joe: Hut, two, three, four *[turns, stops when he sees Pete]*. Good morning, Pete.

Pete: Good morning, Joe. I'm here to take over for you.

Joe: Good. I'm really beat!

Pete: How was your night? Anything happen?

Joe: You won't believe it! Some crazy guy named Daniel refused to obey the king's new law. Babylon News was here awhile ago—reporting LIVE from the Lion Pit! And of course, that attracted a lot of attention! Before we knew what was going on, a crowd gathered, and I thought we'd never break it up! Things didn't calm down until around four in the morning!

Pete: So what's the deal? Why'd this guy, Daniel, break the law anyway?

Joe: It's really ridiculous! The king's new law says that no one can pray to any god or man except the king. They are only trying the law out for a month to see how well it goes! This guy was just plain dumb—he should've just played along, but no—he has to go and defy the king by praying to his God in front of an open window for all the world to see!

Pete: That does sound pretty dumb! Some people just don't have any sense!

Joe: Yeah, like praying to one god instead of another makes any difference!

Pete: And like anyone would think there was a god or a man more powerful than the king!

Joe: Or that anyone would dare disobey him!

Pete: It's ridiculous!

Joe: Outrageous!

Pete: Idiotic!

Joe: Absurd!

Pete: Mush for brains!

Joe: Lion chow! *[Both laugh.]*

Pete: Well, at least those news people are gone. I don't think they'll be back this morning, do you?

Joe: Naw—the guy's been devoured by now. There won't be anything left of him to interview. There's not going to be any more excitement around here today.

Pete: Another fool bites the dust, eh?

Joe: Looks that way. Or in this case, the lions are doing the biting! Well, I'm outta here. See you later. Too bad you missed all the excitement.

Pete: Yeah. See you later, Joe.

Daniel enters, walking toward the two soldiers, humming to himself. The soldiers turn to face him.

Daniel: Good morning!

Both: Good morning! *[Turn and look at each other and then back at Daniel.]*

Joe: Hey! Aren't you—? You're, you're—that guy! Daniel! The one who was thrown to the lions!

Daniel: That's right!

Joe: But, but—you're still alive!

Daniel: That's right! God very kindly decided to shut the mouths of the lions—we all spent a very restful night together! *[Pause.]* Beautiful morning, isn't it? Have a nice day!

Daniel exits. The two soldiers turn back toward each other.

Pete: "God decided to—" Oh man! I think you and I have been praying to the wrong god!

Joe: I think you're right!

Pete: Whew! We'd better find out more about this God of Daniel's! I'm going right now to talk to him!

Joe exits. Pete begins to march.

Pete: Hut, two, three, four *[turns in opposite direction].* And as soon as I get off duty, I'm going to join you! Hut, two, three, four *[turns in opposite direction].*

Digging Deeper

Why did Daniel refuse to obey the king's law?

Do you think Daniel should have obeyed the law in order to avoid punishment? Why?

What did the people of Babylon learn when God shut the mouths of the lions?

How can we be more like Daniel?

Crisis at Nineveh

Scripture: Jonah 1–4

Characters: King of Nineveh, Simmons (the king's aide)

Props/Costumes:
- King wears sackcloth—coarse, dark, unadorned clothing.
- (optional) Rub flour on king's head and face and hands.
- Simmons wears a aluminum foil suit with a brightly colored piece of yarn attached to shoulder (make the suit by wrapping foil around the puppet's body, allowing holes for his arms).

Script

King paces back and forth looking for something.

King: *[calling out]* Simmons! Simmons? Where are my forms for issuing a decree to the country?

Simmons: *[enters looking down at his suit]* They're right there on your table, sir. I saw them last—*[as Simmons lifts his head and sees the king, he stops abruptly. The king turns from the table and sees Simmons. They speak together.]*

King & Simmons What's that you're wearing?!

King: As you can see, Simmons, I'm wearing sackcloth. What are you wearing?

Simmons: This is a disaster suit, sir. I had one made for you, and one for me. And if you don't mind my saying so, sir, you better get yours on! Jonah said we had only forty days until God destroys Nineveh. And a week has gone by already! We're running out of time!

King: *[patiently]* What, exactly, is a disaster suit, Simmons?

Simmons: *[looks at his suit again]* It's made from fireproof cloth—in case God sends fire from the sky! And if I pull this string on my shoulder, it will inflate into a giant life preserver—just in case God sends a flood. Isn't it ingenious? I put yours in your chamber, sir.

King: Well . . . it certainly is unusual. But I don't think that a "disaster suit" is the answer to our problem. Jonah said the reason God is going to destroy Nineveh is because of the wickedness here. Don't you think we should listen to him and repent? That's what I've done—which is why I'm wearing sackcloth and have been sitting in the ashes.

Simmons: Oh my king, what do we really know about this man, Jonah? Do you think he was really sent from God with this message?

King: Yes, Simmons, I believe he was—and I want to issue a proclamation to the entire country.

Simmons: A proclamation? What do you wish to say?

King: Instead of getting ready for the destruction of our city, we need to repent, and ask God for forgiveness.

Simmons: But why should we have to do that? You're a good king and an all-around nice guy! In fact, our city is filled with nice people! We may not be perfect, but we're not really wicked sinners, are we?

King: According to the God of Israel, we are. We have been worshiping other gods and sacrificing to them. I know you are a kind and good man, but being good isn't enough. We all sin—and our constant sinning has caused God to become angry with us. We must ask the God of Israel—the only real God—to forgive us and then we have to repent and change our ways! Don't you see this is the right thing to do?

Simmons: Well, yes, but . . .

King: I want to do what's right in God's eyes so he will be pleased when he looks at me. This is my advice to you as well. Let's call the city to repentance.

Simmons: *[pauses a few moments and then quietly speaks]* Yes, sir, you are right. I'll go get the papers to write up your proclamation.

King: Thank you, Simmons.

Simmons: *[looks down at his suit]* Well, I guess there's no reason to be walking around in a "disaster suit" anymore is there?

King: No, Simmons, no reason at all. From everything that I've heard about the God of Israel, he is compassionate, and slow to become angry. If we are truly sorry for what we've done, and change our ways, perhaps the Lord God will spare our city.

Simmons: Let's hurry and tell the people what we need to do!

King: Yes, let's hurry.

They exit together.

Digging Deeper

What happened to Jonah before he got to Nineveh that showed God's willingness to forgive people who repent?

Do you think that the king made a good decision when he asked the people to repent and stop sinning? Why?

What can we learn about God's forgiveness from this story?

The Mysterious Star

Scripture: Matthew 2:1-6

Characters: Wise Man #1, Wise Man #2, Amos (their servant)

Props/Costumes:
- The wise men are dressed in royal clothing, with turbans, crowns, etc.
- Servant is dressed in plainer, biblical clothing.
- Water pistol filled with water to squirt over stage for "camel spit" (optional)

— Script —

Wise Man #1 enters and looks up toward the sky. After a few moments, Wise Man #2 enters, looks at Wise Man #1 and then looks in the same direction.

W M #2:   I've never seen anything like this before! It's amazing!

W M #1:   Yes, it is. *[Pause.]* You know, I was just thinking. We've been following this star for quite some time now. Do you think we're on the right track?

W M #2:   Yes—I believe so. We are almost to Jerusalem—and it's possible that we'll find him when we get there.

W M #1:   And if not, maybe the city leaders can tell us where to look for him. I'm sure they are all aware of this big event!

Amos enters.

Amos: Excuse me, sirs. We've made camp for the night, and dinner is ready.

W M #2:   *[looks at Amos]* Thank you, Amos. Is everything ready for tomorrow? We have a long day of riding before we'll arrive in Jerusalem.

Amos: Yes, sir. Everything has been arranged just as you asked, but we are having a bit of trouble with one of the camels. He's been restless and every time I go near him, he spits at me!

Shoot water pistol over stage toward the audience to activate "camel spit."

Amos: There he goes again! *[Speaks toward backstage area:]* Now cut that out! *[Looks at Wise Man #2 and sighs.]* I'm sorry, sir. I just don't know what to do with him!

W M #1:   It's OK, Amos. Maybe he just needs a good night's sleep—like the rest of us. I'm sure he'll be fine tomorrow.

Amos: Yes sir. *[Pause.]* May I ask you a question?

W M #1: Certainly, Amos. What is it?

Amos: I was wondering—why have you not used maps instead of following this star day after day?

W M #2: We are looking for someone, Amos, and we don't know exactly where he is.

W M #1: That's why a map wouldn't be much use at this point. We believe we are being led by this star.

Amos: But who are you looking for?

W M #2: We are looking for a baby—a baby born to be the king of the Jews.

Amos: Why do you want to find him?

W M #2: Because we believe he has been sent by God—

W M #1: —and we want to find him so we can worship him.

W M #2: And we might find him tomorrow—when we arrive in Jerusalem!

W M #1: That's why we want everything to be ready—the gifts we brought, the clothes we are going to wear—

Amos: All this fuss just for a little baby? [Shakes his head.] I don't get it.

W M #1: This is not just any baby, Amos. This is a king.

W M #2: And this is not just any king. He is a king who has been sent by God.

W M #1: A divine delivery!

Amos: [repeats thoughtfully] A divine delivery. A king sent by God. I think this is going to be a very interesting trip! May I ask you one more thing?

W M #2: Certainly, Amos. What is it?

Amos: When you find him, do you think that I could see him too? And worship him with you?

W M #1: You're on this trip with us, aren't you? And you're helping us find him?

W M #2: Of course you will see him too—and you can worship him with us!

W M #1: This king will be like no other king you have ever seen—

W M #2: —like no other king who has ever lived!

Amos: Wow—and we will find him all because of a star!

W M #1:   That's right. Now let's go have our dinner so we can get some sleep. We've got a big day ahead of us tomorrow!

All exit together.

Digging Deeper ───────────────

Why did the wise men feel more secure following the star than using maps?

What did they find when they arrived at the palace?

They wanted to worship Jesus because they knew he was a king. Should we feel the same way?

My Idea of Heaven

Scripture: Revelation 21:1–22:5

Characters: Bart Gibbons (interviewer), Monica, Steve, Jennifer

Costumes/Props:
- All wear modern clothing.
- Bart has a microphone (can be made by taping a Styrofoam ball to the top of a dowel and taping or pinning it to the puppet's hand).

Script

Bart enters with microphone in his hand.

Bart: *[to audience]* Hello, everyone! This is Bart Gibbons coming to you LIVE from the streets of _____ *(name of your town)!* We're out here today to ask people what they think Heaven will be like! Here comes someone now! *[Monica enters from stage right. Bart turns toward her.]* Excuse me, miss—we're out here for a special interview and want to know, What do you think Heaven will be like?

Monica: Oh! Well . . . my idea of Heaven is to never have to work again! If I lived in Heaven, I'd be able to sit and watch TV all day and have people bring me lemonade and chocolates and ice cream!

Bart: But those are all things that could happen here on earth. Don't you think Heaven will be more special? More unusual?

Monica: Well—no. I don't think Heaven is really that much different from earth. I don't think anyone really knows for sure what it will be like.

Bart: Uh, well, thank you for your comments. *[Turns to his right.]* Oh, uh—here comes someone else. Sir! Sir! May I have a word with you? *[Monica exits stage left as Steve enters stage right and approaches Bart.]* Sir—we are doing a special interview for our television audience, and I was wondering if you could share with us what your idea of Heaven is—what do you think Heaven will be like?

Steve: *[shrugs]* I don't know. I've never really thought about it.

Bart: You've never thought about it? Not even once?

Steve: Nope. I don't really believe in Heaven. I don't even think it's a real place! It's all a fantasy—like Never-Never Land! Now, if you'll excuse me, I'm late for work.

Bart: Uh, sure—thank you for your comments. *[Steve exits quickly stage left. Jennifer enters stage right. Bart speaks to audience:]* Well, let's try another person, shall we? *[Turns toward Jennifer.]* Oh miss—could I have a moment of your time?

Jennifer:	Yes? What can I do for you?
Bart:	My name is Bart Gibbons, and I'm interviewing folks on the streets of _____ *(name of your town)* today to find out what their idea of Heaven is. Can you tell our audience what you think Heaven will be like?
Jennifer:	Well, according to the Bible, it's going to be a place where there will be no more death or sadness or crying or pain.
Bart:	How interesting! Then you believe that Heaven is a real place?
Jennifer:	Of course Heaven is a real place! It's just difficult to imagine a place where things are so much better than they are here on earth. Just think, no more pain—not even a headache! It's kind of hard to imagine, isn't it?
Bart:	Well, yes, but—how can you be so sure that Heaven will be like that?
Jennifer:	Because the Bible says so. And the Bible also says that because Jesus gave his life to pay for our sin, we will be able to go there to be with him one day!
Bart:	One day? When will that day be?
Jennifer:	Well, no one knows exactly, but Jesus said he is coming back soon! And if we believe in him and accept him as our Savior, he has promised to take us to live with him in Heaven—forever! No one has a hope of going to Heaven without Jesus! *[Pause.]* How about you, Bart? Do you have this hope? Have you accepted Jesus?
Bart:	Well, I can't say I've ever really . . . I'm not sure if . . . well, I . . .
Jennifer:	Do you want to?
Bart:	*[pause and think]* Well . . . YES! Yes I do! Hang on just a second . . . *[to audience]* Thanks for joining us today for this special interview about Heaven! I'm going to find out more about what Heaven is really like—and how I can get there! So long! *[To Jennifer:]* Now, about that other thing . . . there really won't be any more sadness or crying there?

Bart and Jennifer exit together as he is saying the last line.

Digging Deeper ━━━━━━━━━━━━━━━━━━━━━━━

What do you think will be the greatest thing about Heaven?

What kinds of things will not be in Heaven?

What are some ways we can let others know about Heaven and how they can go there?

Don't Worry!

Scripture: Exodus 12–14

Characters: Moses, Gershom, Aaron, Zipporah, Caleb

Costumes/Props:
- All characters wear Biblical dress.
- Sign saying "Several days later . . ."

Script

Four characters enter stage right in single file with Moses in the lead, followed by Aaron, Zipporah, and then Gershom. After they have entered, they should remain facing left, single file, and walking in place.

Aaron: I can't believe it! I still can't believe that the king let us go! You don't suppose it's some kind of trick, do you, Moses?

Moses: All I know is that God has made a way for us to leave and he will take us to the promised land! He will take care of us! Don't worry!

Aaron: But, what if the king changes his mind and sends his soldiers to capture us?

Zipporah: Oh Aaron! We've been traveling for days and days! If the king was going to chase after us, he'd have caught up to us by now! Don't worry!

Gershom: The king is the least of my worries! I'm hungry! When are we going to eat?

Zipporah: Soon, Gershom, soon. *[Pause.]* You know, Moses, I've been thinking. Are you sure we will have enough food to get us where we are going?

Moses: God has taken care of us so far. He will provide. Don't worry!

Aaron: You know, Moses, we are out here in the desert where there is no protection for miles and miles! What about wild animals—like hyenas?

Gershom: And what about poisonous snakes?

Moses: God will take care of us. Just think about what he has done so far! For one thing, because of the plagues he sent, we are free!

Zipporah: Yes! And he caused our Egyptian neighbors to give us gold and silver items, and clothing for the journey!

Gershom: And the sheep and goats and cows too! Could I have some milk?

Moses: And remember, Aaron! *[Looks/points up.]* We follow this pillar of cloud that God sent to guide us every day! God has taken care of us so far, and he will be with us the rest of the way!

Zipporah: And don't forget the fire in the sky at night—it has helped us to see our way so we could keep going! So don't worry, Aaron. God knows what he is doing! Now, let's stop for a while, Moses. The children are hungry and we could all use a break.

Moses: OK. Let's take a break. *[Calls back.]* Hold up!

All exit stage left. Hold up sign which says: "Several days later . . ." Puppets enter in same order. When Moses gets to the middle, he stops; the others bump into him.

Gershom: Hey! What's the big idea?!

Other puppets peek around Moses to see what he's looking at.

Zipporah: Is that the ocean?

Aaron: No—it's the Red Sea. Nothing but water for miles and miles! What do we do now? This can't be our destination!

Caleb enters from stage right (behind Gershom) and passes the other puppets.

Caleb: Moses! Moses! The men on lookout at the end of the caravan have sent me to report that they've spotted the king and his men! They are coming after us!

All: OH NO!

Zipporah: Now I'm worried! Moses, what are we going to do?!

Aaron: I can't believe this! Moses, what have you done?! You've brought us all out here to die!

All begin to shout at once in confusion.

Moses: Everyone listen to me! Don't be afraid! Stand still and see the Lord save you today! You will never see these Egyptians again after today. You will only need to remain calm. The Lord will fight for you.

Zipporah: OK, Moses. You are right. We will do whatever God says we must do and trust him to take care of us. *[Pause.]* What do you want us to do?

Moses: Start walking toward the water. You are going to see how God takes care of his people no matter what! Let's go!

All exit after Moses.

Digging Deeper

How did the people of Israel feel when they saw the sea ahead of them and the army behind them?

Do you think it was hard for them to trust God when they couldn't see any way out?

Have you ever been in a situation that seemed hopeless? Was it hard for you to trust God?

Why can we believe that God will take care of us, no matter what?

Eyewitness Account

Scripture: Matthew 28:1-10

Characters: Joe Friday, Mary, Lydia, Micah, Hosea

Costumes/Props:
- Joe Friday wears modern clothing with hat and/or badge.
- Other characters all wear Biblical clothing.

Script

All puppets enter stage left. Have them stand as if in a huddle and talk excitedly among themselves. Joe Friday enters from stage right and approaches the crowd.

Joe: Alright! Alright! What's going on here?

Crowd opens up and Micah turns toward Joe Friday.

Micah: May I help you?

Joe: Friday's the name. Joe Friday. I've been sent over from police headquarters to investigate—something about a missing body.

Micah: Oh yes! Isn't it wonderful?

Joe: Uh, wonderful? What's so wonderful about a missing body?

Micah: It's Jesus! His body is gone from the grave! He isn't there anymore!

Joe: Yes, well, that's what I'm here about. Weren't a couple of guards posted out here last night?

Micah: Yes, but—well, maybe you should talk to Mary—she was the first to arrive this morning.

Mary: *[turns away from crowd and joins conversation]* Yes! It was around dawn and I was coming down the path when all of a sudden the earth started to shake!

Joe: Yes, yes—and then what happened?

Mary: Well, I looked up and saw an angel coming down from Heaven! And then he rolled the stone away from the entrance to the tomb!

Joe: Uh, are you sure about that? Are you sure it wasn't just a large man?

Mary: Of course I'm sure! I know what I saw—and it wasn't a man! How could a man float down from Heaven? Besides—that rock was way too big and way too heavy for any one man to push it aside!

Joe: Well, what about the soldiers who were guarding the tomb? Were they around? Did they see this, uh, angel too?

Mary: Yes! And they were so terrified that they fainted!

Joe: The soldiers fainted?! Then what happened?

Mary: The angel spoke to me and told me not to be afraid. He said he knew I was looking for Jesus, but Jesus was not in the tomb any longer—he had risen from the dead just as he said he would!

Micah: It's true! It's really true! Jesus has risen from the dead!

Crowd cheers and shouts, "It's true—Jesus has risen from the dead!"

Joe: Now, let's not be too hasty about all this. If the body is missing, someone must have taken it. Once we find the body, we'll be able to clear up this whole matter!

Micah: Well, I'm afraid if you're looking for a body, you're out of luck!

Mary: Yes! There is no body here! And you won't find one either—Jesus is alive!

Joe: Yes, but unless there is an eyewitness who actually saw him alive, we have no real proof!

Mary: But I am an eyewitness! After the angel spoke to me, I ran to tell Jesus' disciples the news! And as I was running away from the tomb, I saw Jesus!

Joe: OK—so this man who looked like Jesus—you saw him and then . . .

Mary: No—it was Jesus! He said to me, "Don't be afraid. Go and tell my brothers to go on to Galilee. They will see me there."

Joe: Yes, well, this all sounds very interesting, but how can you be so sure this was really Jesus—and not just someone who looks like him?

Micah: Because we know Jesus! And because he told us this would happen! He said he would rise from the dead!

Joe: When?

Micah: Before—before any of it happened! Before he was crucified, he said he would rise again—and he did, just as he said he would!

Joe: Yes, well, I would like to talk to these other witnesses—these other followers of Jesus who were supposed to see him in Galilee. Where can I find them?

Mary: They will be meeting together this afternoon—we are all going to get together for a time of rejoicing and celebration over this wonderful news! You are welcome to join us if you like!

Joe: Yes—I, uh, think I may find the answers I need there.

Micah: Yes, Mr. Friday, I think you probably will.

All exit together.

Digging Deeper

How do you think Mary felt when Jesus died?

How do you think she felt when she saw Jesus alive again?

If you had been one of the witnesses, how would you have reacted when you saw Jesus alive again?

Why did God put these eyewitness accounts in the Bible?

Pure and Simple

Scripture: Ephesians 4:25-32

Characters: Ashley, Austin

Costumes/Props:
- Both characters wear modern clothing.
- Small towel for Austin's neck
- Bucket of water
- Small bottle of soap to blow bubbles

Script

Skit begins with Austin singing backstage. Have someone splash water in the bucket while he is singing.

Austin: *[singing]* This is the day this is the day that the Lord has made, that the Lord has made . . . *(or any praise song you choose).*

Austin continues singing as Ashley enters stage right. She looks around and then stage left. Blow a few bubbles up over stage.

Ashley: *[calls out]* Austin! What are you doing in there?

Austin: *[calls from offstage; continue splashing]* I'm taking a bath.

Ashley: *[calls back]* What?! You never take a bath unless Mom makes you—and you never take a bath in the middle of the day! What's going on?

Blow a few more bubbles over the stage and keep splashing water.

Austin: I'm getting holy!

Ashley: *[looks at audience]* Getting holy?! Austin—you're not making any sense! Now once and for all, tell me what you're up to!

Austin: Hang on—I'll be right out!

Austin enters with hair mussed and towel around his neck.

Austin: OK, Ashley! The bathroom's all yours if you want it.

Ashley: Now what's all this about getting holy?

Austin: Well, in Sunday school today, our Scripture verse said that we should be holy like God is holy. And I didn't understand what "holy" meant, so I asked my teacher, Mrs. Wilson.

Ashley: And what did she say?

Austin: She said that to be holy means to be pure. I still didn't get it and was going to ask her again, but before I could, John Anderson got sick and she had to take him to his mother.

Ashley: That still doesn't explain why you're taking a bath in the middle of the day!

Austin: Well, when I got home, I looked up the word pure in the dictionary and it says pure means to be free of dirt or to be clean!

Ashley: OK—now you're beginning to make sense. Austin, that was pretty good thinking to go to the dictionary for more information, but I'm afraid that taking a bath isn't going to make you holy.

Austin: What do you mean? Holy means pure and pure means clean! Sounds pretty simple to me!

Ashley: Well, the Bible tells us what we need to do to be holy—and in a way, it does mean to be clean, but it has to do with what's inside us, not what's on the outside!

Austin: OK—so how do we become holy on the inside?

Ashley: Well, we obey God's Word and live as he wants us to. In Ephesians, Paul says that we should honor our father and mother, always tell the truth, and only say things that are helpful to others. And he says not to steal, not to say hurtful things out of anger—and to be kind and loving to each other.

Austin: All that? That's a lot to remember! But I can see how doing those things would please God.

Ashley: Yes! If we live the way God wants us to, and try to please him by obeying his Word, we will be living a holy life! It doesn't come from taking a bath or washing off dirt—it comes from what you do to obey his Word!

Austin: Yeah, I get it! That makes a lot more sense! Ashley, I'm really glad you told me this! *[Pause.]* Oh no!

Ashley: What is it?

Austin: I can't believe it! I took a bath for nothing!

Ashley: Well, we could go play outside . . . then you're bound to get dirty again!

Austin: Naw—I'd just have to take a bath again tonight. I don't want this one to go to waste! How about playing video games instead?

Ashley: OK.

They exit together.

Digging Deeper

Even though we can never be perfect, as God is, he tells us to be holy. How can we be holy?

Why does God want us to be holy?

Ephesians 4:25-32 lists at least ten ways to be holy. How many can you find?

If everyone in the world tried to be holy, would the world be a different kind of place? Describe what it would be like.

Only One Way Out

Scripture: John 3:16, 17

Characters: Nathan (offstage through entire skit), Max, Julie

Costumes/Props:
• All characters wear modern clothing.

———— Script ————

Skit opens with Nathan offstage calling for help.

Nathan: Help! Help! Somebody help me! Please!

Max and Julie enter from stage right and look around as if trying to find where the voice is coming from. Then Max looks down and to his left and calls to Nathan.

Max: Hello? Hello down there!

Nathan: Who's there?

Max: My name is Max—and my friend Julie is here too! What's your name?

Nathan: Nathan. Can you help me? I'm stuck and I can't seem to get out of here!

Max: How long have you been stuck in there?

Nathan: If feels like forever! I've tried everything to get myself out, but the harder I try, the deeper I seem to go! What is this stuff—quicksand?

Max: I'm afraid not. It's worse than quicksand—it's sin.

Nathan: Sin! How can I be stuck in sin! I'm not some murderer or anything—I'm a nice guy! Sure, I make mistakes now and then, doesn't everybody? But sin—naw! You must be mistaken! This has to be quicksand!

Max: *[to Julie]* Does this sound familiar?

Julie: Uh-huh!

Max: *[to Nathan]* Look—If I could pull you out, I would! But I simply can't do it—it wouldn't work if I tried!

Nathan: But how do you know?

Max: Because not too long ago, I was exactly where you are. And so was Julie!

Nathan:	Well, how did you get yourself out of this?
Julie:	We didn't—there was nothing we could do. We tried and tried to pull ourselves out like you've been doing, but nothing worked!
Nathan:	Then what did you do? Please tell me—and hurry! I'm in this stuff up to my neck and if I don't get free pretty soon, I'm going to die!
Julie:	There's only one way out of there—
Max:	—and only one who can save you! His name is Jesus!
Nathan:	Jesus? Really? OK—will you go get him and ask him to come rescue me?
Max:	*[shakes his head]* That's not necessary.
Julie:	You can ask him yourself—right where you are—and he will save you.
Max:	You see, Nathan, that stuff you are stuck in is not something physical, like quicksand, it's something spiritual called sin. And human power or effort won't do a bit of good in getting you out. The only way to be free of sin is to ask Jesus to forgive you and set you free.
Nathan:	But what can Jesus do? Why is he the only one who can rescue me?
Julie:	Because he is God's Son. You see, we've all been where you are—stuck in sin. And we were all doomed to die because of it. But then, God sent his Son, Jesus—who had never sinned—to earth to die in our place! And now we have the free gift of eternal life because he gave his life for us!
Nathan:	Wow—that's amazing! But why? Why did he do it?
Max:	Because God loves us. That's why he sent Jesus. It's really that simple!
Julie:	So, the first thing you have to do is believe that Jesus is the Son of God. Then you need to accept him as your Savior, and ask him to forgive you—then you will be free!
Nathan:	That's all? I don't have to do some stuff first to be a better person?
Max:	You can't earn your way out, Nathan. That's like pulling yourself out! There's nothing you could do that would be good enough anyway!
Nathan:	OK—I really want to be forgiven—and free from this sinful mess I've gotten myself stuck in! *[Prays.]* Dear Jesus, please hear my prayer and forgive me! I do believe you are God's Son! Thank you for coming to earth and giving your life so I don't have to die for my sin! Please save me and set me free!
Max:	*[watching with amazement]* Here he comes! Isn't that amazing?
Julie:	Yup. Happens every time! Jesus is willing to save everyone who asks!

Nathan: *[calls up]* Hey! I'm—look—I'm out! I'm free! I feel like a new person!

Max: Hey Nathan! Wait up! We've got a lot more great stuff to tell you about Jesus!

Julie: Yeah! This is only the beginning!

Max and Julie exit together stage left.

Digging Deeper

Even though this is a symbolic story about sin, how does it describe what happens in our lives?

Why is "being good" not enough to bring us salvation?

Why is Jesus the only one who can save us?

Lost & Found

Scripture: Luke 15:1-7

Characters: 4 sheep puppets, shepherd

Props/Costumes:
- Sheep puppets (these can be made from tube socks, wiggly eyes, pom-poms, and pieces of felt for ears, nose, and mouth)
- Sign reading "The Next Day"

Script

All four sheep enter bleating: "baa, baa."

Sheep #1: *[turns to the right]* Hey, I think I see a wolf over there!

All others: *[look in same direction]* Where? Where?

While sheep are looking off to one side, the shepherd enters from opposite side of stage.

Shepherd: Hey you guys, how come you're not eating?

All sheep except Sheep #1 turn to look at shepherd.

Sheep #2: We've grazed here all day! There's nothing left!

Shepherd: Well, I found a really good spot over on the other side of the hill. Follow me!

All sheep except Sheep #1 exit after the shepherd. Sheep #1 is still looking for the wolf.

Sheep #1: That's strange. I was sure I saw a wolf! *[Looks around.]* Hey! Where did everybody go? *[Pause.]* OK you guys, very funny! You can come out now. *[Pause.]* Guys? This isn't funny! Come on, quit fooling around! *[Looks at audience.]* This has to be a joke. They wouldn't leave me alone on purpose, especially with a wolf . . . out . . . there . . . somewhere . . . . *[Frightened:]* Guys! Wait! Come back! Don't leave me! *[Runs off-stage.]*

Hold up sign, "The Next Day"; slowly lower the sign. Sheep #1 enters crying.

Sheep #1: I want my shepherd! I've looked and looked for him and for the other sheep, and I can't find them anywhere! I'm cold and I'm hungry and I can't believe they just left me out here alone!

Sheep #1 puts his head down and cries; after a moment, the shepherd enters.

Shepherd: Oh there you are! I've been looking for you everywhere! Are you OK?

Sheep #1: *[rushes over to the shepherd and leans on him]* Oh, Shepherd! I'm so glad you found me! *[Pulls away from shepherd.]* Hey! How come you guys went off and left me out here all alone?

Shepherd: We didn't leave you—you didn't follow! Didn't you hear me tell everyone to follow me to the other side of the hill?

Sheep #1: *[sniffs]* Well, no. I thought I saw a wolf and I was looking to see if I could spot him, and when I turned around everyone was gone! I was so afraid—I thought you had left me and I'd never see you again!

Shepherd: Oh, little sheep, don't you know I would never leave you out here all alone and in danger? As soon as I saw you were missing, I left the rest of the flock to find you. I've been searching for you all night.

Sheep #1: You were out looking for me all night?

Shepherd: Of course! I care about you, and will always look after you. I will always be here when you need me.

Sheep #1: Shepherd?

Shepherd: Yes?

Sheep #1: Thanks for coming to find me. I'm kinda hungry. Can we catch up with the others and get something to eat?

Shepherd: Sure. Just stick close to me, this time, OK?

Sheep #1: Don't worry! I'm right behind you!

They exit together.

Digging Deeper

Have you ever been lost and afraid no one would find you?

What are some ways that we are like sheep?

How is Jesus like the good shepherd in the story?

What does it mean to have Jesus as our Good Shepherd?

Giant Expectations

Scripture: 1 Samuel 17:34, 35

Characters: Eliab, Abinadab, Shammah, David

Props/Costumes:
- Biblical costumes

Script

Scene opens with all three of David's brothers peeking above edge of stage.

Eliab: I can't believe it! He's so big!

Abinadab: Now that's what I call a giant!

Shammah: Do you think he can see us?

Eliab: He's coming this way! Duck!

All three duck suddenly behind stage and then slowly come back up, peeking over the edge again.

Abinadab: Whew! That was close!

Shammah: You can say that again!

Abinadab: Whew! That was close!

Eliab: I hear no one has come forward to fight him yet. The king is still waiting for someone to volunteer.

Shammah: Well, it looks like it's going to be a long wait.

David enters.

David: *[in a loud voice]* HEY! WHY IS EVERYONE HIDING?

Brothers jump and turn suddenly, startled by David's arrival.

Brothers: *[all together]* SHHHH!

Eliab:` What's the matter with you!? Do you want him to see us?

David: Who? You mean that big, ugly guy out on the field? He is going to see me pretty soon. I'm going to fight him—but I brought you your lunch first.

Brothers pause and then burst into laughter.

Abinadab: Yeah, right! That's a good one!

Shammah: Yeah! Little brother, Davey, is going to fight the giant!

Brothers laugh again.

David: Well, I mean it! I am going to fight him. I can't believe no one has volunteered yet.

Eliab: Now stop kidding around, little brother! Going up against this guy would be suicide! You'd be dead meat!

David: But don't you get it? I was almost dead meat before! Remember when that bear attacked my flock?

Abinadab: Yeah, I thought you were a gonner!

David: I thought I was a gonner too. But when I saw that bear taking off with one of our father's sheep, I went after it and killed it—not because I was so strong, but because God was with me. He gave me strength to do it. And since God helped me kill a bear, he can help me defeat this giant too!

Shammah: Well, I think you're crazy!

Eliab: Don't do it, David. You can't go out there against this guy all alone!

David: Don't worry, I'll be back for lunch. Besides, I won't be going out there alone.

David exits. Brothers slowly duck back down behind the stage as they exit.

Digging Deeper

What did David mean when he said he wasn't going to fight the giant alone?

How could David be sure God would be with him?

How can we be sure that God will be with us in difficult times?

Tell about a time when God helped you (or someone you know) through a difficult situation.

The Reluctant Dipper

Scripture: 2 Kings 5

Characters: Naaman, Messenger

Props/Costumes:
- Make spots out of yellow clay or construction paper and attach to Naaman's face with straight pins or tape.
- Drape a hood over Naaman's head so his face is not visible; attach a piece of string to back of the hood so it can be pulled off easily from behind.
- Both Naaman and messenger wear Biblical dress.

Script

Naaman enters, with hood pulled forward on his head so you can't see the spots on his face. He raises his hand as if knocking on a door. (Make knocking sound backstage when he is knocking.) Messenger comes to answer the door.

Messenger: Yes, what is it?

Naaman: *[clears throat]* Ahem! Yes—I am Naaman, commander of the army of the King of Aram! Please show my servants where they can park my chariot—and please let Elisha the prophet know that I am here to see him!

Messenger: What do you want from him?

Naaman: *[pull string on back of hood so it falls off]* I need to be healed.

Messenger: *[gasps]* How dare you come here?! You'll infect us all! Go away!

Naaman: Please, sir! Elisha is my last hope—I must ask Elisha to pray to God to heal me! I've come so far—won't you please ask him to come out and touch me so I can be healed?

Messenger: *[gruffly]* Well . . . wait here and I'll go ask him. And don't touch anything!

Messenger exits. Naaman paces a few moments.

Naaman: *[talking to himself while pacing]* I wonder how he will heal me. Maybe he has some special treatment, or a pill I can take! Or maybe he just has to say a prayer over me, or put his hand out and touch me . . . so this horrible disease will leave me. *[Messenger returns. Naaman speaks excitedly:]* Well, what did he say?

Messenger: He said to tell you . . .

Naaman: Yes, yes?

Messenger: to go to the Jordan River and dip in it seven times.

Naaman: *[surprised]* What!? Wait just a minute! I traveled a long way to be here—I thought Elisha would come out and pray for me or touch me or do something so I could be healed! I expected him to at least come out here and talk to me!

Messenger: Well, I guess you expected wrong. See ya. *[Turns to leave.]*

Naaman: Wait a minute! Maybe you just misunderstood the instructions! Are you sure that's what he said?

Messenger: Sure I'm sure! Don't you think I can understand directions?!

Naaman: Won't you please go back and ask him again? Just to make sure? And be sure you mention that I'm Naaman, commander of the army of the King of Aram, OK?

Messenger: *[sighs loudly]* Oh, alright! Wait here!

Messenger exits. Naaman paces a few moments.

Naaman: *[talks to himself while pacing]* Dip in the Jordan River?! There has to be some mistake! *[Messenger returns. Naaman speaks anxiously:]* What'd he say? Is he coming out?

Messenger: No. The message is the same. I told you I heard it correctly the first time!

Naaman: And did you tell him that I'm Naaman, the—

Both: "commander of the army of the King of Aram." Yeah, yeah, I told him—again!

Naaman: I just don't understand this!

Messenger: Look pal, if I were you, I'd just do it. What have you got to lose?

Naaman: But who knows what's swimming around in that river! And what if it doesn't work? What if I don't get healed?

Messenger: Well, you'd be no worse off than you are now.

Naaman: *[sighs]* You're right about that. *[Pause.]* I guess it's worth a try. It couldn't hurt. In fact, this might be the most important bath of my life!

Naaman exits. Messenger exits in opposite direction.

Digging Deeper

Why was Naaman reluctant to go wash in the river?

Has God ever answered one of your prayers in a way you didn't expect?

Does God ever ask us to do things that are hard to do?

Jerusalem News Network

Scripture: Mark 11:1-11

Characters: Sam Sloan (news anchor), Rhonda Reynolds (reporter), Simone (eye-witness), extras to make crowd noises

Props/Costumes:
- Sam and Rhonda wear modern clothing.
- Mr. Simone wears biblical clothing.
- Poster board TV to hold up in front of Rhonda Reynolds
- (Optional) Microphones attached to each puppet's hand

——— Script ———

Sam Sloan enters.

Sam: This is Sam Sloan, reporting LIVE for the Jerusalem News Network. Tonight we bring you news of a riot in Jerusalem! A man named Jesus, a native of Bethlehem, arrived in the city earlier today to the shouts of a cheering crowd! While the mob appears to be friendly, the leaders in this city are worried that the presence of this man could be the cause of a revolt among the people! We now bring you a live update from our field reporter, Rhonda Reynolds.

Sam looks to his left as Rhonda "floats up" with poster board TV in front of her. She should be positioned far to the left of Sam. Choose a few kids ahead of time to be "shouting" backstage while Rhonda is speaking. Instruct them to shout: "Hosanna—Blessed is he who comes in the name of the Lord!" Be sure they are heard but do not overpower Rhonda's voice.

Rhonda: *[looking straight ahead as she speaks]* Thank you, Sam. As you can hear, the crowd is going wild tonight over the arrival of this man known as Jesus. The streets everywhere are covered with palm branches that people have pulled from trees and waved to welcome him to their city.

Sam: Rhonda, tell us, is it true that the city leaders are worried about a revolt taking place because of this man?

Rhonda: Well, Sam, many of the citizens do believe that this man is the Son of God. They are prepared to follow him no matter what. Of course, many of those in power here have stated that this man is a fraud—and are prepared to take action against him if necessary.

Sam: What type of action is being discussed, Rhonda?

Rhonda: Well, that's not quite clear at this point, Sam. We will be watching throughout the next few days to see what happens here and will keep you up-to-date on events as they take place. For the Jerusalem News Network, this is Rhonda Reynolds reporting.

Sam:　　　　Thank you, Rhonda.

Rhonda "floats" down with the poster board TV until out of sight behind stage.

Sam:　　　　*[to audience]* We have with us today an eyewitness to the amazing event taking place in Jerusalem. Mr. Simone from Bethphage has followed the crowd today—and has actually played a part in Jesus' return to Jerusalem!

Mr. Simone enters.

Sam:　　　　*[turns toward eyewitness]* Mr. Simone, thank you for being with us. Can you tell us what happened with your animals earlier today?

Simone:　　Well, it was pretty strange, for sure! I was in town, see—my hometown, Bethphage, which isn't too far away—and I left my donkey and her colt tied up outside the market, see? And when I came out, some of my friends were standing there looking kinda funny, and my animals were gone!

Sam:　　　　Oh no! Were they stolen?

Simone:　　Well, no. My friends told me that a couple of Jesus' disciples started untying the donkey and colt, and when my friends asked them what they thought they were doing, the disciples said, "The Lord needs them."

Sam:　　　　And your friends just let them take your animals? Some friends!

Simone:　　Well, now, don't go gettin' too upset. See, most of us around here have seen Jesus perform miracles, and we all know of someone who has been healed. Now, my friends wouldn't let just anybody borrow my animals, but they had a feeling that if Jesus needed them, it would probably be OK. And I feel the same way. It's quite a honor to know that Jesus is riding my colt into Jerusalem!

Sam:　　　　Speaking of Jerusalem, what do you think about the excitement there? Do you think it might lead to a revolt?

Simone:　　Well, I don't know anything about a revolt. All I know is Jesus claims to be the Son of God, and because of all I've seen him do, I believe he is!

Sam:　　　　Well, thank you, Mr. Simone, for your eyewitness account leading up to today's events!

Mr. Simone exits.

Sam:　　　　That's our news report for today. Thank you for joining us. This is Sam Sloan reporting for the Jerusalem News Network!

Sam exits.

Digging Deeper

Why were the people in Jerusalem cheering for Jesus as he came into the city?

Why were some of the religious leaders upset by this?

How is the fact that Jesus came to earth good news for us?

How can we celebrate this good news today?

Miraculous Sighting!

Scripture: John 6:16-21

Characters: Ned (a fisherman), Ted (another fisherman with a bad cold)

Props/Costumes:
- Each puppet wears either a fisherman's cap or a rain hat.
- Attach a tissue to Ted's hand with tape or a pin.
- Create a boat out of brown poster board and have a person backstage hold it up in front of the puppets as they move.
- (Optional) Attach two dowels with strings to the boat to be fishing poles.
- (Optional) Tape of surf sounds

Script

Ned and Ted enter within the boat. Ted should talk as if his nose is stuffed up.

Ted: Ah, ah, ah, AH-CHOO! *[Wipes nose with tissue.]*

Ned: Bless you.

Ted: Thanks. *[Blows nose.]*

Ned: Sounds like you've got a nasty cold there.

Ted: Yeah. Ah, ah, ah, AH-CHOO! I tried a different kind of medicine this morning, but it's not helping at all.

Ned: You should be home in bed instead of out here in this freezing air!

Ted: Ah, ah, ah, AH-CHOO! *[Wipes nose.]* Got to work, you know. I need to catch something to sell at the market!

Ned: *[looks up at the sky]* There sure is a lot of fog out here tonight—and it looks like it might rain!

Ted: That's all I need! *[Sniff, sniff.]* Ah, ah, AH *[stops sneeze]*.

Ned: Look—why don't you lie down and get some sleep? I'll call you if the fish start biting.

Ted: Nah. I can't breathe if I lie down. Besides, I—ah, ah, ah, AH-CHOO *[wipes nose]*—just want to hurry up and catch some fish so I can go home!

Ned: *[peers out at audience as if looking off in the distance]* Hey—do you see what I see?

Ted: What? *[Blows nose.]*

Ned: Looks like we're not the only ones out tonight. I think that's Pete's boat! But I can't quite be sure—this fog is so thick!

Ted: *[sniff, sniff]* It's hard to see much of anything out there—the fog is too thick and my eyes keep watering. *[Covers eyes with tissue and leans on stage so audience can't see his eyes.]*

Ned: Well, I doubt they're having any more luck than we are tonight! I think the fish have all gone to bed, eh Ted?

Ted: *[snoring]* ZZZZZZZZ . . . . .

Ned: *[still looking out into the distance]* Hey! Wait a minute! I must be seeing things! Or else I'm dreaming! Hey Ted—wake up! TED! WAKE UP!

Ted: What?! What?! Did we catch anything?

Ned: Ted! Look out there, across the lake—what do you see?

Ted: What? *[Sniff.]* Oh, ah, I see Pete's boat—and it looks like his crew is with him. So what?

Ned: Look over there—to the right of the boat! *[Both puppets look to their right.]*

Ted: Where? *[Calmly.]* Oh, you mean that man walking on the top of the water?

Both: *[shout]* A MAN WALKING ON TOP OF THE WATER?!?!

Ted: That's impossible! I must be seeing things! Maybe it's that new cold medicine I took—but wait a minute—are you seeing it too?

Ned: Yeah—maybe we've got some kind of strange condition that comes on fishermen after they've been fishing too long or something! Maybe we are hallucinating!

Ted: No—[sniff, sniff] that can't be! It must be the fog!

Ned: Let's row over there and get a closer look! This must be an illusion! A man can't just walk on water! That would be . . .

Ted: Impossible!

Exit by moving the boat and puppets downward to stage left until out of sight.

Digging Deeper

Who was the person the fishermen saw walking on the water toward Peter's boat?

Why was Jesus able to walk on water? Why don't "the rules of nature" apply to him?

Why did Jesus do miracles when he was here on earth?

The Son Who Left Home

Scripture: Luke 15:11-32

Characters: Narrator, Father, Tom, man on the road, 2 pigs (optional)

Props/Costumes:
- Tom wears a dirty t-shirt with a button-up shirt over it and a pair of sunglasses.
- Later in the script, you will mess up Tom's hair.
- Father and man on the road can both wear modern dress.
- Use pig puppets for 2 pigs (optional).

——— Script ———

Narrator: Once there was a man who had two sons. This man had made a lot of money and had saved it so that when he died, his sons would inherit all that he owned. But the younger son, Tom, decided he didn't want to wait until that day. He wanted his share now.

Father and Tom enter together.

Narrator: So Tom said to his father . . .

Tom: Father, I want my share now!

Father and Tom exit together.

Narrator: So the father divided up all he owned and gave Tom his share. And then Tom left to go on a long trip.

Tom enters wearing sunglasses and walking from one side of the stage to the other.

Tom: *[singing to himself]* What a beautiful day! I'm on my way! No more work for me—I'm gonna play, play, play, every day, day, day! *[Tom exits.]*

Narrator: Well, Tom had a great time spending all his money and having fun. But after awhile, he ran out of money! And soon he didn't have anything to eat—and then he got very, very hungry!

Tom reenters without sunglasses and with his hair messed up.

Tom: I'm so hungry! It's been three days since I've had anything to eat! And my money is all gone! I'd better find a job so I can buy some food or I'll starve!

Man on the road enters.

Man: Hello there!

Tom: *[weakly]* Oh, hello.

Man: You're not from around here, are you? I know everyone who lives in this town, and I've never seen you before.

Tom: My name's Tom. And I'm looking for a job. Do you know if anyone needs some work done?

Man: Well . . . let's see . . . I have been needing a man to help out with some of my farm animals. If you're interested, my place is up the road a bit.

Tom: Yes, I am! Can I start today—right now?

Man: Why sure! Come with me!

Tom and man exit together.

Narrator: Well, Tom went to work for this man and was sent to the field to feed the man's pigs!

Tom enters wearing the t-shirt (no button-up shirt over it). His hair should be messed up.

(Optional): Pigs enter on either side of him with heads looking down and making pig sounds as though they are eating.

Tom: This is terrible! How could I have gotten myself into such a mess?! I'm weak with hunger but I won't get anything to eat until I've cleaned up this pigpen and fed these pigs! I'm so hungry, I could faint! *[Tom looks down as if looking at the pigs' food.]* In fact, I'm so hungry I could eat just about anything! *[Tom pauses and looks down again, then speaks to audience]* WHAT AM I THINKING?! THIS IS RIDICULOUS! Even the hired men on my father's ranch eat better than this! But here I am so hungry that even pig slop looks good enough to eat! I have been very foolish to come all this way and end up like this!

Narrator: Then Tom had an idea.

Tom: I've got an idea! I will go home and ask my father to let me live there and work as one of his servants. I can't expect him to forgive me and still treat me like a son. But maybe he will let me come back and work for him as a hired hand. I hope he won't be angry. I hope he will forgive me and let me come home. *[Tom (and pigs) exit.]*

Digging Deeper

What did the father in our story do when his son came home?

Jesus told this story to teach us what our heavenly Father is like. What do we learn about God from this story?

What is the best thing to do when we make a mistake or a bad decision?

Scripture: Luke 11:5-10

Characters: John (a traveler), Ephraim (the host), Miriam (Ephraim's wife; we hear her voice only), Micah (Ephraim's neighbor)

Props/Costumes:
- All puppets wear Biblical dress.
- John and Ephraim will be "knocking" on imaginary doors during the skit, so they should have rods attached to their arms for movement.
- Sign saying, "KNOCK, KNOCK"

Directions:
- Before skit, instruct the audience that every time they see the "KNOCK, KNOCK" sign, they should knock on their chairs or on the floor
- (Optional) Begin script with lights out; use a flashlight backstage to allow puppeteers to read lines and to show puppets entering as though approaching a house at night.

Script

John enters stage right and walks to center stage. Hold up "KNOCK, KNOCK" sign while John knocks on imaginary door. Lower sign.

Wait a few seconds. Hold up sign again while John knocks on imaginary door. Lower sign.

Miriam: [voice offstage] Ephraim! Someone's at the door.

Ephraim: [voice offstage] Who could it be at this hour? It's after midnight!

Hold up "KNOCK, KNOCK" sign again while John knocks on imaginary door. Lower sign.

Ephraim: [voice offstage] OK, OK, I'm coming! Who could it be at this hour?

Ephraim enters. Turn on lights.

Ephraim: John!

Miriam: [voice offstage] Ephraim! Who is it?

Ephraim: [calls backstage] It's John! [To John] We didn't think you would get here until the day after tomorrow!

John: I've been traveling day and night. I wanted to get here as quickly as I could! I'm so sorry to wake you!

Ephraim: That's no problem! Come on in! You must be exhausted—and hungry!

John: Yes! I ran out of food yesterday and couldn't find a market anywhere!

Ephraim: Follow me—I'll show you where you can sleep!

Exit together. Turn lights out again except for backstage flashlight.

Ephraim: *[offstage—loud whisper]* Miriam, wake up!

Miriam: *[offstage—sleepily]* What? What is it?

Ephraim: *[offstage—loud whisper]* I can't find any bread in the house, and I need to give John something to eat!

Miriam: *[offstage]* We don't have any bread—I'm baking tomorrow.

Ephraim: *[offstage—loud whisper]* But he hasn't eaten since yesterday! I must find him something to eat! *[Pause.]* Miriam?

Miriam: *[offstage—snoring]* ZZZZZZZZZ

Ephraim enters center stage and goes to stage left.

Hold up "KNOCK, KNOCK" sign while Ephraim knocks on imaginary door. Lower sign. Wait a few seconds. Then hold up sign again while Ephraim knocks again on imaginary door. Lower sign.

Micah: *[voice offstage]* WHO IS IT?

Ephraim: It's me—your neighbor—Ephraim!

Micah: *[voice offstage]* WHAT DO YOU WANT?

Ephraim: A friend of mine has come into town to visit me. But I have nothing for him to eat. Please loan me three loaves of bread!

Micah: *[voice offstage]* The door is locked. My children are already in bed. I cannot get up and give you the bread now! Come back tomorrow!

Hold up "KNOCK, KNOCK" sign while Ephraim knocks on imaginary door again. Lower sign. Wait a few seconds. Hold up sign again while Ephraim knocks again. Lower sign.

Micah: *[voice offstage]* GO AWAY, EPHRAIM! I'M NOT GETTING UP!

Ephraim: But Micah—I really need that bread! Please!

Hold up "KNOCK, KNOCK" sign while Ephraim knocks—keep knocking for five seconds. Turn on lights. Micah enters and looks at Ephraim. Lower sign. Knocking should stop.

Ephraim: I'm sorry, Micah, but I really need that bread. I wouldn't bother you if it weren't important! I'll repay you tomorrow after Miriam bakes some more.

Micah: *[sighs]* All right, Ephraim. Come on in and I'll get you your bread.

Ephraim follows Micah offstage.

Digging Deeper ━━━━━━━━━━━━━━━━━━━━━

Why did Micah end up giving Ephraim the bread?

Jesus told this story to teach us about prayer. What did we learn?

At the end of this story, Jesus told the people to ask, seek, and knock. Look up Luke 11:9 to find out what will happen when we do these things.

A Message Without Any Words

Scripture: Psalm 19:1-4

Characters: Carl, Carrie

Costumes/Props:
- Both characters wear modern dress.
- Carl has on a "space helmet" (made by wrapping aluminum foil around his head).

——— Script ———

Carl enters, moving slowly as if floating in space.

Carl: *[talking as if in a spaceship]* Roger, Houston. We are now orbiting the earth and will land on the moon at approximately twenty-one hundred hours.

Carrie: *[enters as Carl finishes his sentence]* Carl—What are you doing!?

Carl: *[talking as if in a spaceship]* Wait! It appears that there is life out here in space! But we're not quite sure whether it's human . . .

Carrie: Carl! It's me—Carrie!

Carl: . . . the life form appears to be able to breathe without life-support . . .

Carrie: Carl! Listen to me! I'm trying to talk to you!

Carl: Uh-oh. The life form is trying to communicate! Houston, I think we have a problem!

Carrie: That does it! I give up! *[Turns to leave, then stops.]* Hey—wait a minute! *[Turns back toward Carl and says in sweet voice:]* Oh, Mr. Spaceman, I guess you won't be able to share any of my chocolate chip cookies out here in space! They would just float away with no gravity! I'll just have to eat them all by myself! *[Carrie turns to leave.]*

Carl: *[in normal voice]* Wait, Carrie! Don't leave!

Carrie: *[turns back toward Carl]* Why were you ignoring me?

Carl: Sorry. I was just caught up in my imagination. We had this really neat video at school today and I saw how the earth looks from outer space. It's totally awesome!

Carrie: So that's why you're out here floating in space!

Carl: Yeah! I was floating and thinking and imagining—and wondering what it must have been like out there when God decided to create the earth and everything. Not just anybody could do that, you know.

Carrie: I know. Remember when we went to the Grand Canyon last year? Now that was pretty awesome! Not just anybody could do that either!

Carl: Yeah—can you imagine God molding all those rocks and mountains and canyons? And it probably only took the strength from his little finger to do it!

Carrie: You know something? There are a lot of ways God's creation shows his greatness—without even saying a word!

Carl: What do you mean?

Carrie: Well, the Grand Canyon is one way. And all the mountains, and the oceans, and—

Carl: —and the sun and stars and moon in outer space!

Carrie: That's right. Without even a word. Remember the Psalm Grandma taught us the other night?

Carl: Yeah—Psalm 19:1-4. *[Recites while looking up:]* The heavens tell the glory of God. And the skies announce what his hands have made.

Carrie: *[looks up]* Day after day they tell the story. Night after night they tell it again.

Carl: They have no speech or words. They don't make any sound to be heard.

Carrie: But their message goes out through all the world. It goes everywhere on earth.

Both are quiet for a few moments.

Carl: *[looks at Carrie]* Hey—I've got a great idea!

Carrie: *[looks at Carl]* What is it?

Carl: Let's go out in the backyard tonight and look at the stars and hear the message without any words all over again!

Carrie: Great idea! *[Pause.]* But do me a favor? Leave the helmet in the house!

Carl: *[as they exit]* What's wrong with the helmet? You don't like my helmet?

Digging Deeper

Which part of creation makes you feel closest to God? Why?

What parts of God's creation show how great he is?

What are some ways we can celebrate God's creative power?

That's Incredible!

Scripture: Genesis 12, 15

Characters: Talk show host, Abraham

Costumes/Props:
- Talk show host should wear modern clothing.
- Abraham should wear biblical clothing.
- Make "starry sky" by painting a large sheet of cardboard black. (It is best to use a large appliance box for this.) Poke holes all over the flat and then insert the small bulbs from white Christmas lights on the back of the flat. Put this behind the puppet stage near an outlet. It will be raised in the darkened room to represent the stars in the sky.
- Poster board sign saying, "Applause"

Script

Host: Hello, everyone and welcome to, "That's Incredible!" We have a guest with us today who is 170 years old, and he has an incredible story to tell us! His name is Abraham. Please help me welcome him to our studio!

Hold up "Applause" sign. Abraham enters.

Host: Hello and welcome to our show.

Abraham: Thank you. I'm glad to be here!

Host: Now, let me ask you first on behalf of our audience—are you really 170 years old?

Abraham: I am.

Host: And is it true that you received word from God when you were about 75 years old, telling you that you would have a son?

Abraham: Well, his exact words at that point were "I will give this land to your descendants." This meant that I needed to begin a family—because I was already 75 and had no children yet.

Host: And did it happen? Did you have a child?

Abraham: Yes, I did—in fact, my son Isaac now has twin sons of his own! Their names are Jacob and Esau. They are so full of energy! And that youngest one, Jacob, is always up to something!

Host: So, your son Isaac was born when you were about 76 years old?

Abraham: Oh no! I didn't have Isaac until many years later.

Host: But I thought God told you—

Abraham: I know, I know. When God told me he was going to give the land to my descendants, I thought my wife and I would have a child right away. But a year passed, and then another and another, and we still had no children. I began to wonder if God had really given me this promise. And then something wonderful happened.

Host: Your wife told you she was going to have a baby!

Abraham: Not quite. God spoke to me again.

Turn out lights in the room and raise flat with lights attached. Plug in Christmas lights.

Abraham: It was a very dark night, but the stars were shining bright. And God said, "Look at the sky. There are so many stars you cannot count them. And your descendants will be too many to count." God made a promise to me that night. And I just knew he was going to do it! But it still took a few more years of waiting before my son was born. And what a baby he was! He had such an appetite!

Lower "stars" and unplug. Turn room lights back on.

Host: So exactly how old were you when your son Isaac was born?

Abraham: I was 100 and my wife, Sarah, was 99. That was a wonderful day!

Host: Well, I'm sure the audience will agree with me when I say: That's incredible! Before we go, tell us, what did you learn most from this experience?

Abraham: That God will always keep his promises—no matter how long it takes!

Host: Well, that's all the time we have for today. Thank you, Abraham, for coming on our show. *[To audience:]* Please join us next time for another exciting episode of "That's Incredible!"

Hold up "Applause" sign as host and Abraham exit.

Digging Deeper

Do you think it was hard for Abraham to believe God would give him a son when he was so old?

Is it sometimes difficult to believe God's promises?

How can we be sure God will always keep his promises?

To Infinity and Beyond!

Scripture: Psalm 90:2, 4

Characters: Tony, Susan

Costumes/Props:
• Both characters wear modern clothing.
• Susan should have a circle of yarn (or an "eternity bracelet") on her wrist.
• Both characters need to be able to make arm movements.

Directions: Before doing this skit, give an 8" length of yarn to each member of the class. Instruct each member to tie the two ends together in a knot to make a circle, and wear it on his wrist during the skit. (If time allows, you may want to have children make an "eternity bracelet" by braiding three strands of colored yarn together.)

Script

Tony enters with his head hanging down, sighs, and leans his head on his arm. Susan enters.

Susan: Hey, Tony, there you are! I've been looking all over for you! Are we going to play with your space station action figures or not?

Tony: No—we can't.

Susan: Why not?

Tony: *[sits up]* Because the batteries that were in them are dead! And those were the kind of batteries that are supposed to keep going and going and going—forever!

Susan: Forever?

Tony: Yeah—to infinity and beyond!

Susan: Oh. I'm sorry. Maybe your mom can take us to get some more.

Tony: No—I already asked. She doesn't have time today. *[Sighs.]* I guess it's true what they say . . . nothing lasts forever.

Susan: Well, that's not exactly true. Maybe some things don't last—like toys and batteries—but there is someone who has always been around: God.

Tony: You know, I always wondered about that. I know God created the earth and the plants and the animals and people and everything else. But I never could figure out who created God!

Susan: That's just it! God existed before anything or anyone else! God is eternal!

Tony:	What do you mean, God is internal?
Susan:	E-ternal. That means "without a beginning or an end, everlasting, timeless."
Tony:	To infinity . . .
Susan:	and beyond!
Tony:	Does that mean that God wasn't born and won't die?
Susan:	Yes.
Tony:	And doesn't have a bedtime?
Susan:	That's right. There is no time in Heaven. That's why it's called eternity.
Tony:	Eternity—is that like infinity?
Susan:	Kind of. The Bible says that, to God, "a thousand years is like the passing of a day. It passes like an hour in the night."
Tony:	*[Pause.]* I'm still not sure I understand.
Susan:	OK. Let's try this; my Grandma showed me by giving me this *[holds up arm]*.
Tony:	A piece of yarn? *[Looks at audience.]* She's talking about a piece of yarn! *[Pause.]* Hey! You guys have pieces of yarn too!
Susan:	Look, Tony *[holds arm out],* it's like this. See this knot? Let's pretend that's the beginning of time, OK?
Tony:	*[watching Susan's arm]* Well—OK.
Susan:	*[to audience]* Now, you guys over there, are you holding onto the knot on your piece of yarn? *[Waits for response, then looks back down at her arm.]* Now move the yarn around in a circle until you get to the end—OK? *[Wait for audience response.]* Everybody got it?
Tony:	*[still looking at Susan's arm]* Okaaaay—
Susan:	Now where are we—at the beginning or the end?
Tony:	Well, the knot was the beginning and the knot is the end.
Susan:	So when you get to the end, you are really at the beginning again—get it?
Tony:	Hey! That's pretty cool! It goes on forever and never ends—just like God! Can I make one of those yarn circles too?
Susan:	Sure—I have some extra yarn over at my house. Let's go! *[Waves to audience.]*

Thanks, everybody, for helping me out!

Tony: *[to audience]* Yeah, thanks!

Both turn to exit—as they leave, Tony says,

Tony: I guess there really is someone who keeps going and going and going . . .

Susan: . . . to infinity and beyond!

They exit.

Digging Deeper

What does it mean to say that, to God, "a thousand years is like the passing of a day"?

How would you explain to a friend that God has no beginning and no end?

How is the timelessness of eternity in Heaven different from our life on earth?

Written in the Clouds

Scripture: 1 John 4:7-10

Characters: Carl, Kim

Costumes/Props:
- Both wear modern clothing.
- (optional) cassette tape of thunder/rainstorm

Script

Carl enters and lies on his back with his head looking up to the ceiling. After a few moments, Kim enters and looks at him.

Kim: Hey Carl! Whatcha doing?

Carl: Looking at clouds.

Kim turns over and lies on her back, looking up at the ceiling. They are quiet for a few seconds.

Kim: Hey—you see that one over there? *[Points up and to her right.]* It kind of looks like an elephant!

Carl: Yeah. And the one next to it kind of looks like an alligator!

Kim: Carl, why are you out here looking at clouds? I thought you were going over to Joey's to ride bikes.

Carl: I changed my mind. I might go tomorrow. Maybe. I don't know.

Kim: But I thought you promised Joey you'd come over today! Don't you want to go?

Carl: Sure, I want to go. But I'm not sure what to do about Joey. The other kids at school think he's a geek. And even though I like him a lot, I don't want the other kids making fun of me! I hate it when the guys make fun of me!

Kim: I know what you mean. When I was in second grade, the other girls made fun of me because my baby teeth still hadn't fallen out. I mean, it wasn't my fault, but they were still mean to me. *[Pause.]* Are you going to stop being Joey's friend?

Carl: *[sigh]* I don't know. *[Points up.]* There's a cloud that kind of looks like Joey.

Both are quiet a few moments.

Kim: You know, I think people are kind of like clouds.

Carl: How come?

Kim: Well, you can see the outside of clouds, but not what's inside them. You know there is water in clouds because when it storms, rain comes out.

Carl: What's that got to do with us?

Kim: Well, you can tell whether or not God is inside of us by what we do on the outside—by our actions. *[Points.]* Hey! That one looks like a big heart!

Carl: Hey look! *[Points to his far right.]* There's one of those planes pulling a banner behind it! What's it say?

Kim: *[reads haltingly]* We should love each other because love comes from God. First John 4:7. Come join us for church this Sunday at . . . at . . . I can't see the rest of it. What a cool idea!

Carl: *[raises upright suddenly]* I've got to go.

Kim: *[raises upright]* Why?

Carl: Because you're right! Because I'm like a cloud with rain inside it! I'm a kid with God inside me. And if God is in me, and love comes from God, then there's love in me too and love wouldn't ditch Joey as a friend—no matter what!

Kim: So you're going over to ride bikes with him after all?

Carl: No—we'll probably play video games instead. *[Looks up.]* It looks like it might rain.

Play tape-recorded thunder as both exit.

Digging Deeper

Has there ever been someone in your life who you thought of the way Carl thought about Joey?

When people seem weird or strange to us, is it OK not to like them?

Have you ever not liked someone and then after you got to know him, you liked him?

When God's Spirit lives inside us, he is eager and able to help us. What are some ways he helps us?

From Prison to Palace

Scripture: Genesis 39–41

Characters: The king, chief officer to the king, Debra (a servant), Joseph

Costumes/Props:
- All wear biblical clothing.
- Chief officer has a piece of brightly-colored string tied around his finger.
- Sign saying, "Back at the Palace . . ."
- Sign saying, "Later That Day . . ."

Script

Chief officer and Debra enter from opposite ends of puppet stage.

Officer: Good morning, Debra. How's everything in the palace this morning?

Debra: Terrible! Absolutely terrible! The king's in a horrible mood!

Officer: Why? What's wrong?

Debra: Word around the palace is that he had a dream last night that really upset him. He's called in all of the palace magicians, but no one can tell him what it means!

Officer: Oh that is terrible news! *[Rubs his head with the hand that has string on the finger.]*

Debra: Hey, why is that string tied around your finger? It seems like you've been wearing it for months! Do you remember why?

Officer: No. I keep trying to remember, but it's no use! It must've been important!

Debra: Well, I've got to go down to the river and do the laundry! See you later.

Officer: See you later, Debra.

Debra exits.

Officer: *[looks at his finger and then suddenly realizes what he's forgotten all this time]* Hey, wait! Now I remember! *[Looks at the audience.]* Ooooh! I've got to get to the palace!

Chief officer exits quickly. Hold up sign saying, "Back at the Palace . . ." Lower the sign. The king enters and begins pacing.

King: What could it mean? I know it's something important! I must find out what my dream was all about!

Chief officer enters timidly.

Officer: Uh, excuse me, sir, but could I have a word with you?

King: *[keeps pacing; does not look at the chief officer]* Not now. I've got something important on my mind! I need peace and quiet!

Officer: But sir, this is important—it's about that dream you had last night.

King: *[stops pacing and looks at the chief officer]* What is it? What do you know about the dream I had last night?

Officer: Well, I heard that you are looking for someone who can tell you what it means, and I think I know someone who can.

King: What?! How can you? I've asked all my court magicians and all of the wise men of Egypt, and none of them can help me! Who do you know?

Officer: Your majesty, about two years ago, you became angry with me and with your baker and you put us both into prison. While we were there, we each had a very strange dream on the same night. There was a young Hebrew man in prison named Joseph, who told us what our dreams meant and things happened exactly as he said they would. He asked me to tell you about him when I came back to the palace—but I'm sorry to say I forgot—until this morning. I think this young man might be able to tell you the meaning of your dream!

King: Quick! Send for him at once! Bring him here and we will see!

Officer: Yes, your majesty.

Chief officer bows and exits quickly. The king exits opposite side. Hold up sign, "Later That Day . . ." Lower the sign. The king enters and continues pacing. Joseph enters.

Joseph: You sent for me, sir?

King: *[looks up]* Hmm? Oh yes—are you Joseph?

Joseph: Yes sir. My name is Joseph.

King: I have had a dream. But no one can explain its meaning to me. I have heard that you can explain a dream when someone tells it to you.

Joseph: I am not able to explain the meaning of dreams. God will do this for the king.

King: Come with me and I will tell you what happened in my dream.

Joseph and the king exit together. Hold up sign, "Later That Day. . ." Lower the sign. Chief officer and Debra enter from opposite ends of puppet stage.

Debra: Is it true? Did the young Hebrew interpret the king's dream? Someone came running down to the river to tell us! Is it true?

Officer: Yes! And you won't believe what else happened! The king has made Joseph second in command over all of Egypt! The king's dream showed that a huge drought is going to come, and Joseph has been put in charge to get things ready so we don't all starve!

Debra: That's amazing! Who would've thought an unknown Hebrew would go from being a prisoner to being the second in command over Egypt—all within a single day!?

Officer: Yes—who would've thought . . . It kind of makes you wonder what else this man is going to do, doesn't it?

Digging Deeper

When Joseph was young, he dreamed that God would make him a great man. Do you think it was difficult for him to believe this when bad things kept happening to him?

How did God use the bad things that happened to Joseph to fulfill his plan for Joseph?

How can we know that God is still in control even when bad things happen to us?

Scripture: 2 Kings 19; 2 Chronicles 32:7, 8

Characters: Hezekiah (King of Judah), assistant to the king, manager of the palace, messenger

Costumes/Props:
- All characters are in biblical clothing.
- The assistant will need a small piece of paper rolled at each end like a scroll and attached to his hand with clear tape or a straight pin.
- Messenger should have a small trumpet taped to his hand; you can use a small plastic toy trumpet or cut one out of poster board.

Directions: Instruct the children to make a trumpet sound (to cavalry "charge" tune) whenever messenger enters and raises his trumpet.

Script

Messenger enters and raises his trumpet. Children respond with trumpet sound. King Hezekiah enters hurriedly with his royal assistant and palace manager.

Assistant: Your majesty, another message has just arrived from Sennacherib, the king of Assyria!

King: Oh no! Not again! Read it to me!

Assistant: It says *[reads from note attached to his hand]*, "Don't be fooled by the god you trust. Don't believe him when he says you will not be defeated by the king of Assyria. You have heard what the kings of Assyria have done. They have completely defeated every country. Do not think you will be saved." *[Lowers note.]* Your majesty, this man is dangerous! His men are outside the city walls making fun of God and humiliating us. He's going to attack our city! We're doomed!

King: *[to messenger]* Quick! Send a message to the prophet Isaiah! Tell him to pray and ask God to help us!

Messenger: Yes sir! Right away! *[He exits.]*

Assistant: *[to the king]* Sir, we must do something about this man! He has defeated armies many times before! I think he means business!

Manager: But maybe he's bluffing! He's probably just trying to scare us.

Assistant: Have you forgotten what he did when he attacked Judah before? He is dangerous! We can't take any chances. We need to come up with a strategy of our own to discover what he is planning to do.

Manager: OK, but what can we do? *[Pause.]* Wait—I've got it! The P.D.F.! The Palace Detective Force can begin an investigation and question anyone who has any information about this man!

Assistant: Wait! Wait! Spies—we need to get a team of spies to go and sneak into Sennacherib's palace! They can go undercover—as a cook, or a gardener—or something! Then we can find out what he's going to do!

Manager: That's a great idea! What do you think, your majesty?

King: I think there is no point in sending in the P.D.F. or any spies. There is only one who knows what this man is going to do, and that is the Lord our God. We've asked Isaiah to pray, and now we must also pray and ask God for help.

All exit. Messenger enters and raises his trumpet. Children respond with trumpet sound. King Hezekiah enters again with his royal assistant and palace manager.

Assistant: Your majesty, another message has arrived; it's from the prophet Isaiah.

King: Yes, what does he say?

Assistant: *[reads from scroll attached to hand]* The prophet Isaiah says, "This is what the Lord says about the king of Assyria: 'He will not enter this city. He will not even shoot an arrow here. He will not fight against it with shields. He will not build a ramp to attack the city walls. He will return to his country the same way he came.' The Lord says, 'I will defend and save this city.'"

King: Gentlemen, we have our answer. The Lord has declared what will happen.

Manager: But sir, everyone is scared to death! And King Sennacherib still has his men posted outside the city walls, tormenting the people with his threats!

King: Then it's time to make an announcement. It's time to tell our people not to be afraid. We do not have to fear this man because God has already told us what is going to happen. It's time to declare once and for all *[kingly declaration]* we will trust in the Lord our God! Let's go!

All exit together.

Digging Deeper

When someone makes fun of you, or some member of your family, or something that is important to you, how do you feel? Is it hard not to fight back?

King hezekiah was upset when his enemies made fun of God and threatened him, but instead of getting his army together, what did he do? (2 Kings 19:1, 2)

What does this story teach you about God's ability to protect you?

This story also teaches a good way to handle bullies. What is it? (2 Kings 18:36)

Worship Resources

Each of the skits in this book correlates to a unit of worship from Standard Publishing's two-year series of Worship Folders for elementary kids. This series was developed to help children worship God for who he is and what he has done. Each eight-page folder is a thematic unit with Scripture activities, music, prayer suggestions, and small group ideas for four sessions of children's worship.

Listed with each skit title below is the correlating Worship Folder and its order number.

Divine Assignment
Jesus Is Immanuel (42251)

The Incredible View
Jesus Is God's Son (42252)

Do You Have an Appointment?
Jesus Is Our Friend (42246)

Dangerous Decision
God, the Only God (42260)

Crisis at Nineveh
God Is Forgiving (42243)

The Mysterious Star
Jesus Is Messiah (42257)

My Idea of Heaven
Jesus Is Our Hope (42256)

Don't Worry!
God Is Our Caregiver (42248)

Eyewitness Account
Jesus Is Alive (42255)

Pure and Simple
God Is Holy (42263)

Only One Way Out
Jesus Is Savior (42253)

Lost & Found
Jesus Is Our Shepherd (42249)

Giant Expectations
God Is Ever-Present (42245)

The Reluctant Dipper
God Is Powerful (42242)

Jerusalem News Network
Jesus Is Good News (42261)

Miraculous Sighting!
Jesus, Miracle Doer (42259)

The Son Who Left Home
Jesus Is Love (42262)

The Persistent Neighbor
Jesus Is Our Teacher (42258)

A Message Without Any Words
God Is Creator (42241)

That's Incredible!
God Is a Promise Keeper (42247)

To Infinity and Beyond!
God Is Eternal (42244)

Written in the Clouds
God Is Inside Us (42264)

From Prison to Palace
God Is Sovereign (42250)

Trust in the Lord Our God!
God Is All-Knowing (42254)